Oprah's
THE LIFE
YOU WANT
PLANNER

HOW TO USE THIS PLANNER

WHEEL OF LIFE AND VISION BOARD:

Before diving in, use these tools to reflect on your life and dreams as they currently stand. What needs to change to help you reach your goals?

FILL IN THE BLANKS:

Start anytime you want! Fill in the days/months to match whenever you begin your journey.

FOCUS PAGES:

What does each theme mean to you? Answer the reflection questions and determine how you can best incorporate each focus into your life.

INTENTION:

Identify your motivation for the week. Why do you do the things you do? What do you want the end result to be?

DONE LIST:

Track and celebrate any time you complete an important task.

WEEKLY REFLECTION:

Use the prompts to assess your progress each week. Think about what you've achieved and what you'd like to do next.

For more inspiration and guidance on how to make living well a daily practice, visit OprahDaily.com.

© Oprah Daily LLC 2021

Oprah Daily and *Oprah's The Life You Want* are trademarks of Harpo, Inc.

FOUNDER AND EDITORIAL DIRECTOR, OPRAH DAILY: **Oprah Winfrey**
EDITOR AT LARGE, OPRAH DAILY: **Gayle King**
GENERAL MANAGER, OPRAH DAILY: **Alison Overholt**
CREATIVE DIRECTOR, OPRAH DAILY: **Adam Glassman**
CONTRIBUTING EDITOR: **Lindsay Flader**

CREATIVE DIRECTOR, HEARST PRODUCT STUDIO: **Gillian MacLeod**
MANAGER, HEARST PRODUCT STUDIO: **Missy Steinberg**

INTERIOR PHOTOGRAPHY: © Ruven Afanador/Harpo, Inc.: 4, 284, 288; © Mitch Boeck/EyeEm: 168; © Jonathan Cyr/500px Prime: 278; © dj_aof/iStock: 196; © Daniela Duncan/Moment: 130; © Aaron Foster/The Image Bank: 40; © Darrell Gulin: 254; © Mario Guti/E+: 186; © Chris Hackett: 260; © ICHIRO/DigitalVision: 10; © Michael Kittell/The Image Bank: 136; © Marser/Moment: 242; © P. Medicus/Moment: 98; © Mia Minor: 58; © Milamai/Moment: 280; © Namthip Muanthongthae/Moment: 232; © NNehring/E+: 220; © Isabel Pavia/Moment: 148; © Gary John Norman/The Image Bank: 272; © Micha Pawlitzki/Corbis Documentary: 118; © Nora Sahinun/EyeEm Premium: 52; © Manuela Schewe-Behnisch/EyeEm: 70; © Schon/Moment: 14; © Joern Siegroth/Moment: 88; © Steve Smith: 154; © taden/iStock: 174; © TakakoWatanabe/iStock: 208; © thethomsn/Moment: 76; © Tatsiana Volskaya/Moment: 100; © Enrico Tricoli/Moment: 112; © TorriPhoto/Moment: 8; © wat/iStock: inside paper jacket; © Westend61: 156; © Moritz Witter/EyeEm: 218

Library of Congress Cataloging-in-Publication Data is on file with the publisher.

ISBN 978-1-956300-00-0

2 4 6 8 10 9 7 5 3   hardcover

HEARST

Oprah's
THE LIFE
YOU WANT
PLANNER

EMBRACE A FULLER LIFE!

I've been keeping a journal since I was 15 years old. When I was younger, my journals were mostly a record of everything I was thinking and feeling at that moment—crying about boys, writing bad poetry, worrying about my weight, or wondering what other people thought of me. In my 40s, I began to use my journals to focus on gratitude, writing lists of what brought me pleasure or joy every day, and it didn't take long to feel a massive shift. By taking a moment to pause and focus on the abundance of my life, I began to notice just how much good there really was.

I know that for many people finding time to journal can be a challenge. It's easy to get caught up in the "busy-ness" of life: rushing from here to there to make this appointment or that meeting, shuttling the children between school and soccer practice, trying to get dinner on the table or carve out some time to meet a friend for coffee. The days, weeks, and months pass in a blur, without a moment to stop, take a breath, and just be. That's why our team at Oprah Daily created this planner.

Within these pages you'll find space to organize appointments and stay on task, alongside thoughtful writing prompts to encourage you to pause and reflect on what really matters in your life. We hope it serves as a practical tool to help you manage your day-to-day schedule as well as a guide to inspire and motivate you to become the best version of yourself. The first thing you'll notice is that we've left the entire planner undated—so no matter where you are or what's in front of you, today is always the perfect day to begin. We've also divided the planner into 12 different sections, each with a specific focus: values that I believe are essential to expanding our heart space and allowing us to step into the fullness of our authentic selves. Every focus lasts four to five weeks, allowing you time to dig deep and cultivate real, lasting change. As you answer the corresponding questions, define what each focus means to you and let it be your guide as you move closer to creating the life you want. You'll also notice several "Ask Yourself" thought-starters—short, simple questions designed to spark ideas and keep you aligned with the current focus. Instead of a to-do list, celebrate everything you accomplish by adding it to the Done List whenever you complete a big task.

Whether you tackle each of the 52 weeks consecutively or start and stop as needed, don't forget to look back and see your progress along the way. It's astonishing to be able to track your own evolution—who you were and who you can still become. We all have a limited number of years on earth. What will you do with yours?

Oprah

The Wheel of Life

The Wheel of Life is a useful tool to help you step back and assess what areas of your life give you satisfaction and what areas could use a little more attention. Review the categories on this page then rank your satisfaction with each category on a scale of 1 (dissatisfied) to 10 (fully satisfied). When you look at your completed wheel, ask yourself: How does this make me feel? Which areas need the most improvement? What's one small step I can take to get started?

INTEGRITY: Living an authentic life where your beliefs and actions align. Being true to yourself and the values you cherish.

VULNERABILITY: Your willingness to be open and share emotions, thoughts, and feelings, even when it may be painful or embarrassing.

CONNECTION: The quality of relationships in your life. Do you feel part of a community with the people around you? Do you freely give and receive love?

BEING FULLY PRESENT: Your ability to live in the present moment without dwelling on the past or worrying about the future.

RESILIENCE: Your ability to overcome challenges and adversity.

COMPASSION & EMPATHY: How would you rate the amount of kindness, patience, and understanding you show to others? To yourself?

FORGIVENESS: Your ability to let go of grudges or unresolved feelings toward yourself or others.

RENEWAL: Your ability to take care of your own physical and mental health and give yourself time to rest and recharge.

SERVICE: Your contribution to the world. How often do you take the chance to serve?

GRATITUDE: Giving thanks and celebrating all the good people, places, and things in your life, no matter how simple or small.

JOY: How satisfied you are with the amount of happiness, peace, and contentment in your life.

REFLECTION: Your ability to pause and examine your life, assess the progress you've made in achieving your goals, and decide what you want for your future.

These categories represent the 12 focuses you will work through over the course of this planner. Return to this page and assess your growth when you've completed all 52 weeks.

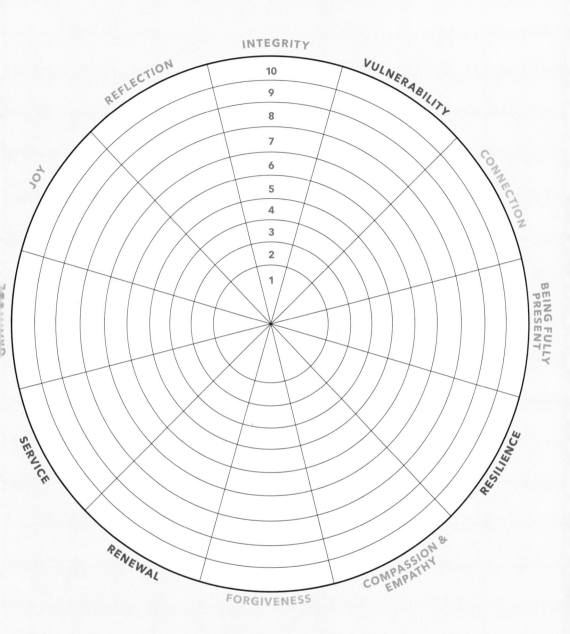

INTEGRITY

VULNERABILITY

REFLECTION

CONNECTION

JOY

10
9
8
7
6
5
4
3
2
1

BEING FULLY PRESENT

SERVICE

RESILIENCE

RENEWAL

COMPASSION & EMPATHY

FORGIVENESS

SETTING YOUR
YOUR
INTENTION

I first learned about intention back in the 1980s when I read Gary Zukav's "The Seat of the Soul." It was a transformational lesson for me—one that changed how I move through the world, how I operate my business, and who I choose to work with. Gary wrote, "Every action, thought, and feeling is motivated by an intention, and that intention is a cause that exists as one with an effect. If we participate in the cause, it is not possible for us not to participate in the effect. In this most profound way, we are held responsible for every action, thought, and feeling, which is to say, for our every intention." Today, anyone who knows me knows that intention is still the number one principle that rules my life. It stems from the greatest spiritual law: What you put out into the world is what you get back. I don't do anything without first asking, "What is my intention?"

In order to step into the most powerful version of yourself, you need to know not just what you want, but why you want it. Throughout this planner, you'll have a chance to set your own intention at the start of each week. Do you want to be more present? More loving? How can you move through the world while honoring your why? Start living from your intention, and watch your life unfold in all the ways you want.

—Oprah

Creating Your
Vision Statement

I was raised with this biblical teaching from Proverbs 29:18: *"Where there is no vision, the people perish."* I used to recite that verse in Sunday school, but it wasn't until I was much older, trying to manage a business and my life, that I clearly understood its meaning: Having a vision creates a path for the future. It focuses you and allows for clarity moving forward. You decide where you want to go, who you want to be, and, as Paulo Coelho says in *"The Alchemist,"* *"When you want something, all the universe conspires in helping you to achieve it."* What do you want? When you can specifically and fully answer that question, you begin to create a roadmap for what your heart desires.

—Oprah

What would my ideal life look like?

_____

_____

_____

_____

_____

_____

_____

What kind of person do I want to be in that life?

_____

_____

_____

_____

_____

_____

What gives me a sense of meaning, value, and purpose?

_____

_____

_____

_____

_____

_____

_____

What can I do now to start moving in the direction of achieving what I say matters?

_____

_____

_____

_____

_____

_____

VISION BOARD

Ask yourself, "When I see my life one year from now, what does it look like?" Think about areas of your life you really want to change—in your family, relationships, hobbies, fitness, well-being, or finances. What words and images come to mind?

Use this page to write, draw, or paste whatever inspires your vision of the future: your dreams, your goals, and your ideal life. Put your vision into the universe, then prepare yourself to meet it as you create your future. *Return to this page throughout the year to remind yourself of your dreams.*

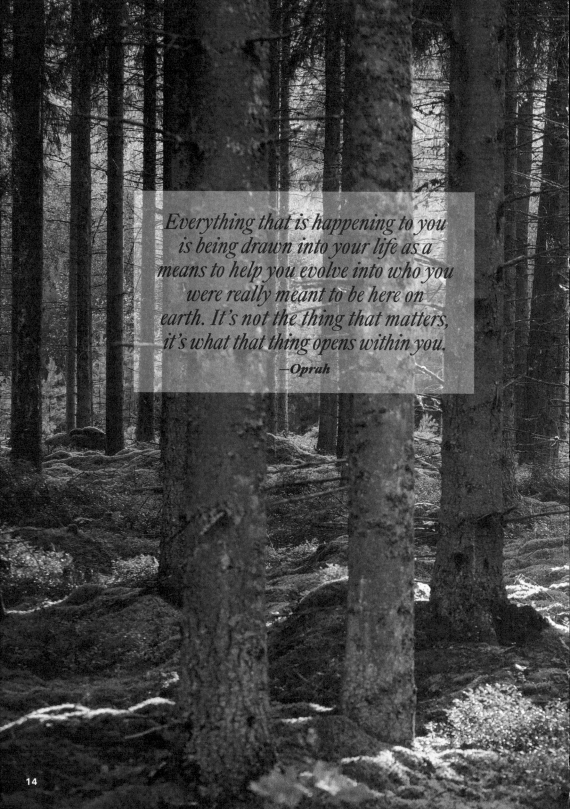

Everything that is happening to you is being drawn into your life as a means to help you evolve into who you were really meant to be here on earth. It's not the thing that matters, it's what that thing opens within you.

—Oprah

SUNDAY	MONDAY	TUESDAY	WEDNESDAY

THURSDAY	FRIDAY	SATURDAY	Notes

MONTH 2 //

SUNDAY	MONDAY	TUESDAY	WEDNESDAY

THURSDAY	FRIDAY	SATURDAY	Notes

MONTH 3 //

SUNDAY	MONDAY	TUESDAY	WEDNESDAY

THURSDAY	FRIDAY	SATURDAY	Notes

SUNDAY	MONDAY	TUESDAY	WEDNESDAY

THURSDAY   **FRIDAY**   **SATURDAY**   **Notes**

MONTH 5 //

SUNDAY	MONDAY	TUESDAY	WEDNESDAY

THURSDAY	FRIDAY	SATURDAY	Notes

SUNDAY	MONDAY	TUESDAY	WEDNESDAY

THURSDAY	FRIDAY	SATURDAY	Notes

SUNDAY	MONDAY	TUESDAY	WEDNESDAY

THURSDAY	FRIDAY	SATURDAY	Notes

SUNDAY	MONDAY	TUESDAY	WEDNESDAY

THURSDAY	FRIDAY	SATURDAY	Notes

SUNDAY	MONDAY	TUESDAY	WEDNESDAY

THURSDAY	FRIDAY	SATURDAY	Notes

SUNDAY	MONDAY	TUESDAY	WEDNESDAY

THURSDAY   **FRIDAY**   **SATURDAY**   **Notes**

MONTH 11 //

SUNDAY	MONDAY	TUESDAY	WEDNESDAY

THURSDAY   **FRIDAY**   **SATURDAY**   **Notes**

MONTH 12 //

SUNDAY	MONDAY	TUESDAY	WEDNESDAY

THURSDAY **FRIDAY** **SATURDAY** **Notes**

Integrity

Of all the values I hold dear, integrity is everything to me. I always thought it meant doing the right thing no matter what. But recently my friend Martha Beck deepened my understanding of what integrity really means. It's about alignment. In order to find the truest expression of ourselves, we must be in alignment with the truth. Everyday things you do—telling little white lies, gossiping, not standing up for yourself—knock you off-balance. When you are out of alignment, your goals become more difficult to reach. The beauty of living with integrity means that life becomes simple: We never have to spend time or energy questioning ourselves because our beliefs and actions work in perfect harmony. In the coming weeks, take a moment to think about how you can live in alignment and better embody your highest integrity.

—Oprah

sk yourself the questions below. Whether you express yourself by writing, drawing, or pasting,
t your answers help shape your intention in the weeks ahead.

What does the word *integrity* mean to me?

Who is someone I admire for living their life with integrity?

Am I satisfied with who I am as a person? What do I believe to be true about myself?

Are there areas of my life in which I can be more truthful?

MY INTENTION

Living in alignment with the truth means speaking your truth. **Ask yourself: Am I willing to say what I'm thinking? Why or why not?**

MONDAY /

TUESDAY /

WEDNESDAY /

THURSDAY / _____ _____

_____

_____

_____

_____

_____

_____

FRIDAY / _____ _____

_____

_____

_____

_____

_____

_____

SATURDAY / _____ _____

_____

_____

_____

_____

_____

_____

SUNDAY / _____ _____

_____

_____

_____

_____

We're all familiar with the idea of a to-do list...but do we ever celebrate ourselves for completing it? Use the lines below to write down the tasks you accomplished this week.

My Done List

○ _____

○ _____

○ _____

○ _____

○ _____

○ _____

○ _____

○ _____

○ _____

○ _____

○ _____

○ _____

○ _____

○ _____

○ _____

You become what you believe.

—Oprah

WEEKLY REFLECTION

When was I at my best this week?

_____
_____
_____
_____
_____
_____
_____
_____

When was I true to myself?

_____
_____
_____
_____
_____
_____
_____
_____

What do I want to improve?

_____
_____
_____
_____
_____
_____
_____
_____

What was the most important thing I learned this week?

_____

_____

_____

_____

_____

_____

Notes

_____

_____

_____

_____

_____

_____

_____

_____

_____

_____

_____

_____

_____

_____

MY INTENTION

_____

_____

To live your most authentic life, you must let go of anything that pulls you out of alignment.
Ask yourself: What's one thing I can remove from my life right now that compromises my integrity?

MONDAY / _____

_____

_____

_____

_____

TUESDAY / _____

_____

_____

_____

_____

WEDNESDAY / _____

_____

_____

_____

_____

_____

THURSDAY /

_____

FRIDAY /

_____

SATURDAY /

_____

SUNDAY /

_____

My Done List

○ _____
○ _____
○ _____
○ _____
○ _____
○ _____
○ _____
○ _____
○ _____
○ _____
○ _____
○ _____
○ _____
○ _____
○ _____
○ _____
○ _____
○ _____
○ _____
○ _____

When you want something, all the universe
conspires in helping you to achieve it.

—Paulo Coelho

WEEKLY REFLECTION

When was I at my best this week?

_____

_____

_____

_____

_____

_____

_____

When was I true to myself?

_____

_____

_____

_____

_____

_____

_____

What do I want to improve?

_____

_____

_____

_____

_____

_____

_____

What was the most important thing I learned this week?

_____

_____

_____

_____

_____

_____

_____

Notes

_____

_____

_____

_____

_____

_____

_____

_____

_____

_____

_____

_____

_____

_____

_____

_____

MY INTENTION

Living your life for other people is a sure way to knock yourself right out of alignment. **Ask yourself: Do I seek approval from others when doing certain things? Why or why not?**

MONDAY /

TUESDAY /

WEDNESDAY /

THURSDAY / _____ _____

_____

_____

_____

_____

_____

FRIDAY / _____ _____

_____

_____

_____

_____

_____

SATURDAY / _____ _____

_____

_____

_____

_____

_____

SUNDAY / _____ _____

_____

_____

_____

_____

_____

My Done List

○ _____

○ _____

○ _____

○ _____

○ _____

○ _____

○ _____

○ _____

○ _____

○ _____

○ _____

○ _____

○ _____

○ _____

○ _____

○ _____

○ _____

○ _____

○ _____

○ _____

Peace is your home, integrity is the way to it, and everything you long for will meet you there.

—Martha Beck

WEEKLY REFLECTION *Check-in*

I'm living with integrity by:

I'm looking forward to:

I'm spending the most time:

Three promises I can make to myself are:

I'm reading/watching/listening to:

Notes:

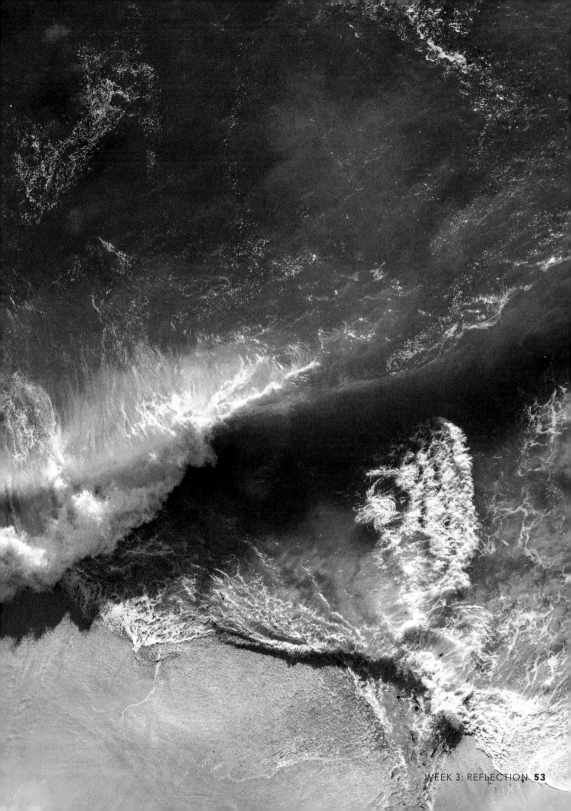

MY INTENTION

Living a life of integrity means telling the truth about ourselves to ourselves. **Ask yourself: What is the real reason that I don't do that thing that I feel deep down I should do?**

MONDAY /

TUESDAY /

WEDNESDAY /

REMEMBER: Every small step matters. Minute by minute, choice by choice, you are getting closer to your goals.

THURSDAY / _____ _____

_____

_____

_____

_____

_____

FRIDAY / _____ _____

_____

_____

_____

_____

_____

SATURDAY / _____ _____

_____

_____

_____

_____

_____

SUNDAY / _____ _____

_____

_____

_____

_____

My Done List

- ○ _____
- ○ _____
- ○ _____
- ○ _____
- ○ _____
- ○ _____
- ○ _____
- ○ _____
- ○ _____
- ○ _____
- ○ _____
- ○ _____
- ○ _____
- ○ _____
- ○ _____
- ○ _____
- ○ _____
- ○ _____
- ○ _____
- ○ _____
- ○ _____

To find yourself,
think for yourself.
—Socrates

WEEKLY REFLECTION

When was I at my best this week?

_____

_____

_____

_____

_____

_____

_____

_____

When was I true to myself?

_____

_____

_____

_____

_____

_____

_____

_____

_____

What do I want to improve?

_____

_____

_____

_____

_____

_____

_____

_____

What was the most important thing I learned this week?

_____

_____

_____

_____

_____

_____

_____

Notes

_____

_____

_____

_____

_____

_____

_____

_____

_____

_____

_____

_____

_____

_____

Vulnerability

*In 2012, I interviewed professor and researcher
Brené Brown for an episode of "Super Soul Sunday."
As we discussed how we can all make our lives
more meaningful through vulnerability, I kept thinking,
"This is everything I know to be true." For me,
being vulnerable really means opening up the heart space.
Your vulnerability and your openness are what
allow you the confidence to know that there's no emotion you
can have that somebody else hasn't had. Vulnerability
is being able to open up your soul and allow other people to
see their souls' reflection in your own. Challenge
yourself to step into the space of vulnerability and open
the door to greater intimacy and connection.*

—Oprah

When have I been too scared to be myself?

When have I gotten hurt for expressing my true feelings?

What is a personal weakness I've never told anybody about?

Who do I admire for being honest about their faults?

MY INTENTION

No experience is ever wasted. Everything that happens to you is helping you become the person you are meant to be. **Ask yourself: What is something I've avoided doing for fear of being vulnerable?**

MONDAY /

TUESDAY /

WEDNESDAY /

THURSDAY / _____ _____

_____

_____

_____

_____

_____

FRIDAY / _____ _____

_____

_____

_____

_____

_____

SATURDAY / _____ _____

_____

_____

_____

_____

_____

SUNDAY / _____ _____

_____

_____

_____

_____

_____

My Done List

○ _____

○ _____

○ _____

○ _____

○ _____

○ _____

○ _____

○ _____

○ _____

○ _____

○ _____

○ _____

○ _____

○ _____

○ _____

○ _____

○ _____

○ _____

○ _____

○ _____

○ _____

You can't get to courage without walking through vulnerability. Period.

—Brené Brown

WEEKLY REFLECTION

What made me feel vulnerable this week? Why?

_____

_____

_____

_____

_____

_____

_____

I was honest about my feelings when...

_____

_____

_____

_____

_____

_____

_____

What am I the most worried about right now? What can I do about it?

_____

_____

_____

_____

_____

_____

_____

How did I show courage this week?

_____
_____
_____
_____
_____
_____
_____

Notes

_____
_____
_____
_____
_____
_____
_____
_____
_____
_____
_____
_____
_____
_____

MY INTENTION

There is freedom in telling the truth about who you are. **Ask yourself: What exactly am I afraid of in sharing my true feelings?**

MONDAY /

TUESDAY /

WEDNESDAY /

REMEMBER: On our journey of self-discovery, we're bound to take the occasional misstep. Every single one of us is a work in progress. Your mistakes do not define who you are.

THURSDAY / _____ _____

_____

_____

_____

_____

_____

FRIDAY / _____ _____

_____

_____

_____

_____

_____

SATURDAY / _____ _____

_____

_____

_____

_____

_____

SUNDAY / _____ _____

_____

_____

_____

_____

_____

My Done List

○ _____
○ _____
○ _____
○ _____
○ _____
○ _____
○ _____
○ _____
○ _____
○ _____
○ _____
○ _____
○ _____
○ _____
○ _____
○ _____
○ _____
○ _____
○ _____
○ _____
○ _____

Your journey begins with a choice to get up, step out, and live fully.
—*Oprah*

WEEKLY REFLECTION

What made me feel vulnerable this week? Why?

_____
_____
_____
_____
_____
_____
_____
_____

I was honest about my feelings when...

_____
_____
_____
_____
_____
_____
_____
_____

What am I the most worried about right now? What can I do about it?

_____
_____
_____
_____
_____
_____
_____
_____

How did I show courage this week?

_____

_____

_____

_____

_____

_____

_____

Notes

_____

_____

_____

_____

_____

_____

_____

_____

_____

_____

_____

_____

_____

_____

MY INTENTION

Opening yourself to others is a risk—but a risk that can lead to love, friendship, and connection.
Ask yourself: With whom do I feel most comfortable sharing vulnerable moments and why?

MONDAY / _____

TUESDAY / _____

WEDNESDAY / _____

THURSDAY / _____ _____

_____

_____

_____

_____

FRIDAY / _____ _____

_____

_____

_____

_____

_____

SATURDAY / _____ _____

_____

_____

_____

_____

_____

SUNDAY / _____ _____

_____

_____

_____

_____

_____

My Done List

○ _____
○ _____
○ _____
○ _____
○ _____
○ _____
○ _____
○ _____
○ _____
○ _____
○ _____
○ _____
○ _____
○ _____
○ _____
○ _____
○ _____
○ _____
○ _____
○ _____

To be alive is to be vulnerable.

—Madeleine L'Engle

WEEKLY REFLECTION *Check-in*

I'm currently feeling:

I'm hoping:

I'm spending the most time:

I'm anxious about:

I'm learning about:

I'm looking forward to:

I'm reading/watching/listening to:

Notes:

MY INTENTION

Being vulnerable means facing our fears of rejection or criticism. **Ask yourself: What is one harsh comment I've received? How did it make me feel?**

MONDAY /

TUESDAY /

WEDNESDAY /

REMEMBER: Permit yourself to feel your emotions. You are allowed to take the time you need to heal.

THURSDAY / _____ _____

_____

_____

_____

_____

_____

_____

FRIDAY / _____ _____

_____

_____

_____

_____

_____

_____

SATURDAY / _____ _____

_____

_____

_____

_____

_____

_____

SUNDAY / _____ _____

_____

_____

_____

_____

My Done List

○ _____
○ _____
○ _____
○ _____
○ _____
○ _____
○ _____
○ _____
○ _____
○ _____
○ _____
○ _____
○ _____
○ _____
○ _____
○ _____
○ _____
○ _____
○ _____
○ _____
○ _____

If we are all able to show our vulnerability, that doesn't mean that you're weak. If anything, I believe, that's probably showing most of your strength.

—Prince Harry

WEEKLY REFLECTION

What made me feel vulnerable this week? Why?

_____
_____
_____
_____
_____
_____
_____
_____

I was honest about my feelings when...

_____
_____
_____
_____
_____
_____
_____
_____

What am I the most worried about right now? What can I do about it?

_____
_____
_____
_____
_____
_____
_____
_____

How did I show courage this week?

_____

_____

_____

_____

_____

_____

_____

Notes

_____

_____

_____

_____

_____

_____

_____

_____

_____

_____

_____

_____

_____

_____

_____

_____

Connection

Over the course of my nearly 40-year career,
I've had thousands of conversations with people from all
over the world. In all that time, no matter whom I'm
speaking to, one common denominator has never changed:
All of us want to know that what we do, what we
say, and who we are matters. Human beings, by design,
desire to connect: to share in a collective experience
and to be in community with one another. In the next several
weeks, take steps to cultivate deeper, more meaningful
connections with the people around you. Open your heart
to love and see it everywhere.

—*Oprah*

What relationships in my life are the most important to me?

What kind of people do I want to surround myself with?

What can I do to show love to the people around me? How can I make them feel valued?

What is one relationship I want to strengthen?

MY INTENTION

_____

_____

Connecting with others begins with identifying who you want to be around. **Ask yourself: What are the most important qualities in a friend, and do I have these qualities?**

MONDAY /

_____

_____

_____

_____

_____

TUESDAY /

_____

_____

_____

_____

WEDNESDAY /

_____

_____

_____

_____

_____

THURSDAY / _____ _____

_____

_____

_____

_____

_____

FRIDAY / _____ _____

_____

_____

_____

_____

_____

SATURDAY / _____ _____

_____

_____

_____

_____

_____

SUNDAY / _____ _____

_____

_____

_____

_____

_____

My Done List

- ○ _____
- ○ _____
- ○ _____
- ○ _____
- ○ _____
- ○ _____
- ○ _____
- ○ _____
- ○ _____
- ○ _____
- ○ _____
- ○ _____
- ○ _____
- ○ _____
- ○ _____
- ○ _____
- ○ _____
- ○ _____
- ○ _____
- ○ _____
- ○ _____

People may not remember what you did or what you said, but they always remember how you made them feel.

—Maya Angelou

WEEKLY REFLECTION

What did I do this week to connect with someone important in my life?

_____

_____

_____

_____

_____

_____

_____

_____

What relationships am I happy with? What relationships am I neglecting and why?

_____

_____

_____

_____

_____

_____

_____

_____

What did I do to connect more deeply with myself?

_____

_____

_____

_____

_____

_____

_____

_____

Who do I want to spend more time with? How will I make it happen?

_____

_____

_____

_____

_____

_____

_____

_____

Notes

_____

_____

_____

_____

_____

_____

_____

_____

_____

_____

_____

_____

_____

_____

_____

_____

_____

MY INTENTION

Holding on to relationships that no longer serve you can block your blessings and keep you stagnant.
Ask yourself: Do the people in my life give me energy and inspire growth?

MONDAY /

TUESDAY /

WEDNESDAY /

REMEMBER: All of us feel overwhelmed at one point or another. Allow yourself the space to focus on the tasks at hand without adding any more to your plate.

THURSDAY / _____

_____

_____

_____

_____

_____

FRIDAY / _____

_____

_____

_____

_____

_____

_____

SATURDAY / _____

_____

_____

_____

_____

_____

_____

SUNDAY / _____

_____

_____

_____

_____

_____

My Done List

○ _____

○ _____

○ _____

○ _____

○ _____

○ _____

○ _____

○ _____

○ _____

○ _____

○ _____

○ _____

○ _____

○ _____

○ _____

○ _____

○ _____

○ _____

○ _____

○ _____

*The chance to love and be loved
exists no matter where you are.*

—Oprah

WEEKLY REFLECTION

What did I do this week to connect with someone important in my life?

_____
_____
_____
_____
_____
_____
_____
_____
_____

What can I do to improve my relationship with _____?

_____
_____
_____
_____
_____
_____
_____
_____

What did I do to connect more deeply with myself?

_____
_____
_____
_____
_____
_____
_____
_____

Am I willing to make compromises in a relationship? If so, what?

Notes

MY INTENTION

It is my belief that we can learn from any situation or any person that shows up in our lives, if only we're willing to listen. **Ask yourself: What's the best lesson I've received?**

MONDAY /

TUESDAY /

WEDNESDAY /

THURSDAY / _____ _____

_____

_____

_____

_____

FRIDAY / _____ _____

_____

_____

_____

_____

_____

SATURDAY / _____ _____

_____

_____

_____

_____

_____

SUNDAY / _____ _____

_____

_____

_____

_____

My Done List

- ○ _____
- ○ _____
- ○ _____
- ○ _____
- ○ _____
- ○ _____
- ○ _____
- ○ _____
- ○ _____
- ○ _____
- ○ _____
- ○ _____
- ○ _____
- ○ _____
- ○ _____
- ○ _____
- ○ _____
- ○ _____
- ○ _____

Love is our true destiny. We do not find the meaning of life by ourselves alone—we find it with another.

—Thomas Merton

WEEKLY REFLECTION *Check-in*

I'm currently feeling connected to:

I'm hoping:

I'm spending the most time:

I'm anxious about:

I'm feeling disconnected from:

I'm looking forward to:

I'm reading/watching/listening to:

Notes:

MY INTENTION

We all need relationships that enrich and sustain us. **Ask yourself: What and who makes me feel loved?**

MONDAY /

TUESDAY /

WEDNESDAY /

HURSDAY / _____ _____

_____

_____

_____

_____

_____

RIDAY / _____ _____

_____

_____

_____

_____

_____

ATURDAY / _____ _____

_____

_____

_____

_____

_____

UNDAY / _____ _____

_____

_____

_____

_____

My Done List

- ○ _____
- ○ _____
- ○ _____
- ○ _____
- ○ _____
- ○ _____
- ○ _____
- ○ _____
- ○ _____
- ○ _____
- ○ _____
- ○ _____
- ○ _____
- ○ _____
- ○ _____
- ○ _____
- ○ _____
- ○ _____
- ○ _____
- ○ _____

Love is when you choose to be at your best when the other person is not at their best.

—Wintley Phipps

WEEKLY REFLECTION

What did I do this week to connect with someone important in my life?

_____

_____

_____

_____

_____

_____

_____

_____

What are my boundaries in a relationship or friendship?

_____

_____

_____

_____

_____

_____

_____

_____

What did I do to connect more deeply with myself?

_____

_____

_____

_____

_____

_____

_____

_____

What did I do this week to show others I love them?

_____

_____

_____

_____

_____

_____

_____

Notes

_____

_____

_____

_____

_____

_____

_____

_____

_____

_____

_____

_____

_____

_____

_____

MY INTENTION

The key to any relationship is communication. **Ask yourself: Do I make an effort to truly listen to the people I care about?**

MONDAY /

TUESDAY /

WEDNESDAY /

THURSDAY / _____

_____

_____

_____

_____

FRIDAY / _____

_____

_____

_____

_____

SATURDAY / _____

_____

_____

_____

_____

SUNDAY / _____

_____

_____

_____

_____

My Done List

○ _____

○ _____

○ _____

○ _____

○ _____

○ _____

○ _____

○ _____

○ _____

○ _____

○ _____

○ _____

○ _____

○ _____

○ _____

○ _____

○ _____

○ _____

○ _____

○ _____

○ _____

Eventually, you will come to understand that love heals everything, and love is all there is.

—Gary Zukav

WEEKLY REFLECTION

What did I do this week to connect with someone important in my life?

_____

_____

_____

_____

_____

_____

_____

_____

Who in my life do I respect the most? Why?

_____

_____

_____

_____

_____

_____

_____

_____

What did I do to connect more deeply with myself?

_____

_____

_____

_____

_____

_____

_____

_____

How do I want others to feel when they are with me? What can I do to make them feel this way?

_____

_____

_____

_____

_____

_____

_____

Notes

_____

_____

_____

_____

_____

_____

_____

_____

_____

_____

_____

_____

_____

_____

_____

*It's really okay to not have all the answers.
The answers will come if you can accept
"not knowing" long enough to get still—and
stay still long enough for new thoughts to
take root in your more quiet, deeper, truer self.
The noise of the world drowns out the
sound of you; **you** have to get still to listen.*

—Oprah

Being Fully Present

I believe being fully present is the sacred jewel in the crown of your life. The ability to slow down and savor the simple pleasures of the present moment is one of my greatest joys. When you are fully present, everything changes. You gain clarity, clear your mind of distractions, and find a new level of calm deep within your soul. As Eckhart Tolle once told me, the only thing you ever have is now. The past is over and the future is not yet here. Our most meaningful moments occur when we slow down, show up, and tune in to what's right in front of us. Begin to embrace the idea of living in the now as a more awakened, vibrant, alive human being.

—Oprah

What is meaningful to me at this moment?

What is a daily ritual that helps bring me stillness?

What distracts me from staying in the present moment?

Who or what could I pay more attention to and why?

MY INTENTION

One of the best ways to center yourself is to focus on your breath. **Ask yourself: Have I focused on my breathing today? Let the air fill your lungs, your heart, your whole being. Exhale. Repeat.**

MONDAY /

TUESDAY /

WEDNESDAY /

THURSDAY / _____

_____

_____

_____

_____

_____

FRIDAY / _____

_____

_____

_____

_____

_____

SATURDAY / _____

_____

_____

_____

_____

_____

SUNDAY / _____

_____

_____

_____

_____

_____

My Done List

○ _____
○ _____
○ _____
○ _____
○ _____
○ _____
○ _____
○ _____
○ _____
○ _____
○ _____
○ _____
○ _____
○ _____
○ _____
○ _____
○ _____
○ _____
○ _____
○ _____

The present moment is the only time over which we have dominion.

—Thich Nhat Hanh

WEEKLY REFLECTION

What was the most meaningful thing I did this week?

_____
_____
_____
_____
_____
_____
_____
_____

How did I practice being fully present?

_____
_____
_____
_____
_____
_____
_____
_____

Was there a time when I could have been more present or aware? What happened?

_____
_____
_____
_____
_____
_____
_____
_____

How can I shift my attention to be more in the moment?

_____

_____

_____

_____

_____

_____

_____

Notes

_____

_____

_____

_____

_____

_____

_____

_____

_____

_____

_____

_____

_____

_____

_____

_____

_____

MY INTENTION

Regular check-ins with your body, mind, and spirit are critical to cultivating awareness.
Ask yourself: How am I feeling in my body, right in this moment?

MONDAY /

TUESDAY /

WEDNESDAY /

THURSDAY / _____

_____

_____

_____

_____

FRIDAY / _____

_____

_____

_____

_____

SATURDAY / _____

_____

_____

_____

_____

SUNDAY / _____

_____

_____

_____

_____

My Done List

○ _____
○ _____
○ _____
○ _____
○ _____
○ _____
○ _____
○ _____
○ _____
○ _____
○ _____
○ _____
○ _____
○ _____
○ _____
○ _____
○ _____
○ _____
○ _____
○ _____
○ _____
○ _____

As long as you are breathing, there is more right with you than wrong with you, no matter what is wrong.

—Jon Kabat-Zinn

WEEKLY REFLECTION

What was the most meaningful thing I did this week?

_____
_____
_____
_____
_____
_____
_____

How did I practice being fully present?

_____
_____
_____
_____
_____
_____
_____

Was there a time when I could have been more present or aware? What happened?

_____
_____
_____
_____
_____
_____
_____

How can I shift my attention to be more in the moment?

_____

_____

_____

_____

_____

_____

_____

Notes

_____

_____

_____

_____

_____

_____

_____

_____

_____

_____

_____

_____

_____

_____

_____

_____

MY INTENTION

How you spend your time defines who you are. **Ask yourself: What requires my focus? How can I give it the full weight of my presence?**

MONDAY /

TUESDAY /

WEDNESDAY /

THURSDAY / _____ _____

_____

_____

_____

_____

_____

FRIDAY / _____ _____

_____

_____

_____

_____

_____

SATURDAY / _____ _____

_____

_____

_____

_____

_____

SUNDAY / _____ _____

_____

_____

_____

_____

_____

My Done List

○ _____

○ _____

○ _____

○ _____

○ _____

○ _____

○ _____

○ _____

○ _____

○ _____

○ _____

○ _____

○ _____

○ _____

○ _____

○ _____

○ _____

○ _____

○ _____

○ _____

Your life is always speaking to you.
The fundamental spiritual question is:
Will you listen?
—Oprah

WEEKLY REFLECTION *Check-in*

I'm currently feeling:

I'm paying attention to:

I'm anxious about:

I'm focused on improving:

Notes:

MY INTENTION

You can't be present if you're stuck looking back! **Ask yourself: What is something from the past I need to let go?**

MONDAY /

TUESDAY /

WEDNESDAY /

HURSDAY / _____ _____

_____

_____

_____

_____

_____

_____

RIDAY / _____ _____

_____

_____

_____

_____

_____

_____

ATURDAY / _____ _____

_____

_____

_____

_____

_____

_____

UNDAY / _____ _____

_____

_____

_____

_____

_____

_____

My Done List

○ _____

○ _____

○ _____

○ _____

○ _____

○ _____

○ _____

○ _____

○ _____

○ _____

○ _____

○ _____

○ _____

○ _____

○ _____

○ _____

○ _____

○ _____

○ _____

The essence of who you are
does not lie in the past. What matters
is what you are willing to do now.

—Eckhart Tolle

WEEKLY REFLECTION

What was the most meaningful thing I did this week?

_____
_____
_____
_____
_____
_____
_____

How did I practice being fully present?

_____
_____
_____
_____
_____
_____
_____
_____

Was there a time when I could have been more present or aware? What happened?

_____
_____
_____
_____
_____
_____
_____
_____

How can I shift my attention to be more in the moment?

_____

_____

_____

_____

_____

_____

_____

Notes

_____

_____

_____

_____

_____

_____

_____

_____

_____

_____

_____

_____

_____

_____

_____

_____

_____

FOCUS 5:
Resilience

*I believe that resilience is the single most important quality that allows human beings to triumph in moments of difficulty. For many people, being resilient means that you can endure hardship and bounce back unscathed. But for me, resilience is really about absorbing the difficult moments, knowing that they've changed you, and moving forward anyway with a resolve to make it through. The truth is, there is no strength without challenge, resistance, adversity, and, very often, pain. It is a blessing to be able to survive and find meaning in each and every hurdle. Think back on your own history—how you got right here, to this moment. Were there events along the way that scared or scarred you? Maybe so. But what's remarkable is that no matter what happened, **you** are still standing, **you** are still here.*

—Oprah

What is the most challenging circumstance that I have ever experienced?

How did that experience change and impact my life?

What aspects of my personality helped me get through that situation?

What did I learn from it?

MY INTENTION

Every challenge we take on has the power to bring us to our knees, but we also all possess the power to stand back up. **Ask yourself: Where in my life have I shown the greatest resilience?**

MONDAY /

TUESDAY /

WEDNESDAY /

THURSDAY / _____ _____

_____

_____

_____

_____

FRIDAY / _____ _____

_____

_____

_____

_____

SATURDAY / _____ _____

_____

_____

_____

_____

SUNDAY / _____ _____

_____

_____

_____

_____

My Done List

○ _____

○ _____

○ _____

○ _____

○ _____

○ _____

○ _____

○ _____

○ _____

○ _____

○ _____

○ _____

○ _____

○ _____

○ _____

○ _____

○ _____

○ _____

○ _____

○ _____

○ _____

I can be changed by what happens to me, but I refuse to be reduced by it.

—Maya Angelou

WEEKLY REFLECTION

How would I rate my mindset this week? How mentally strong do I feel? Why?

_____
_____
_____
_____
_____
_____
_____

What was my biggest accomplishment this week?

_____
_____
_____
_____
_____
_____
_____

What setbacks did I experience this week? How did I respond?

_____
_____
_____
_____
_____
_____
_____

m optimistic about...

_____
_____
_____
_____
_____
_____
_____

Notes

_____
_____
_____
_____
_____
_____
_____
_____
_____
_____
_____
_____
_____
_____
_____

MY INTENTION

True healing, in any capacity, cannot take place until we confront the truth about what happened to us. **Ask yourself: What am I avoiding? Why?**

MONDAY /

TUESDAY /

WEDNESDAY /

THURSDAY / _____ _____

_____

_____

_____

_____

_____

FRIDAY / _____ _____

_____

_____

_____

_____

_____

_____

SATURDAY / _____ _____

_____

_____

_____

_____

_____

_____

SUNDAY / _____ _____

_____

_____

_____

_____

_____

My Done List

○ _____

○ _____

○ _____

○ _____

○ _____

○ _____

○ _____

○ _____

○ _____

○ _____

○ _____

○ _____

○ _____

○ _____

○ _____

○ _____

○ _____

○ _____

○ _____

○ _____

The greatest glory in living lies not in never falling, but in rising every time we fall.

—Nelson Mandela

WEEKLY REFLECTION

How would I rate my mindset this week? How mentally strong do I feel? Why?

_____
_____
_____
_____
_____
_____
_____
_____

What was my biggest accomplishment this week?

_____
_____
_____
_____
_____
_____
_____
_____

What setbacks did I experience this week? How did I respond?

_____
_____
_____
_____
_____
_____
_____
_____

m optimistic about...

_____

_____

_____

_____

_____

_____

_____

otes

_____

_____

_____

_____

_____

_____

_____

_____

_____

_____

_____

_____

_____

_____

_____

MY INTENTION

During difficult times, I often turn to music and prayer to help ease me through whatever challenge I might be facing. One of my favorite anthems for difficult times is Whitney Houston's "I Didn't Know My Own Strength." **Ask yourself: Was there a time I didn't know my strength? What happened?**

MONDAY /

TUESDAY /

WEDNESDAY /

THURSDAY / _____

_____
_____
_____
_____
_____

FRIDAY / _____

_____
_____
_____
_____
_____

SATURDAY / _____

_____
_____
_____
_____

SUNDAY / _____

_____
_____
_____
_____

My Done List

- ○ _____
- ○ _____
- ○ _____
- ○ _____
- ○ _____
- ○ _____
- ○ _____
- ○ _____
- ○ _____
- ○ _____
- ○ _____
- ○ _____
- ○ _____
- ○ _____
- ○ _____
- ○ _____
- ○ _____
- ○ _____
- ○ _____

Always take a moment to celebrate...
the obstacles you've overcome, the silent battles
you've fought, and the hard decisions you've
had to make. Celebrate your strength and resilience.

—Simone Biles

WEEKLY REFLECTION *Check-in*

For me, resilience looks like:

I'm energized by:

I'm hoping:

I'm emotional about:

I'm in control of:

I felt successful when:

Notes:

MY INTENTION

We all need a little inspiration now and then. **Ask yourself: Who is a resilient person that I admire? Why?**

MONDAY /

TUESDAY /

WEDNESDAY /

REMEMBER: Your challenges inspire lessons for you—and everyone around you.

THURSDAY /

_____
_____
_____
_____
_____
_____

FRIDAY /

_____
_____
_____
_____
_____
_____

SATURDAY /

_____
_____
_____
_____
_____
_____

SUNDAY /

_____
_____
_____
_____
_____
_____

My Done List

○ _____
○ _____
○ _____
○ _____
○ _____
○ _____
○ _____
○ _____
○ _____
○ _____
○ _____
○ _____
○ _____
○ _____
○ _____
○ _____
○ _____
○ _____
○ _____
○ _____

There is no such thing as failure.
Failure is just life trying to move us
in another direction.

—*Oprah*

WEEKLY REFLECTION

How would I rate my mindset this week? How mentally strong do I feel? Why?

_____

_____

_____

_____

_____

_____

_____

_____

What was my biggest accomplishment this week?

_____

_____

_____

_____

_____

_____

_____

_____

What setbacks did I experience this week? How did I respond?

_____

_____

_____

_____

_____

_____

_____

I'm optimistic about...

_____

_____

_____

_____

_____

_____

_____

Notes

_____

_____

_____

_____

_____

_____

_____

_____

_____

_____

_____

_____

_____

_____

_____

Compassion & Empathy

*Every day on "The Oprah Winfrey Show," I listened
as thousands of people shared their stories. No matter who
I spoke to or what they talked about, my intention
was always the same: to approach every person with empathy
and compassion. All pain is the same—we just choose
different ways to express it. True empathy comes when you're
able to step out of judgment and understand from
the other person's point of view. Compassion takes it one
step further. Translated from its Latin origin, the
word literally means "to suffer with." You not only feel and
understand someone's pain, you're also moved to help
alleviate it. Extending yourself in compassion to another
human being changes the nature of your relationship—
the acknowledgment of one human being to another is what
bonds, strengthens, and expands the human connection.*

—Oprah

Who is the most empathic person I know? How do they show empathy?

Have I ever had a moment when someone showed me compassion? What happened?

When I show empathy, how does it make me feel?

What does showing compassion look like to me?

MY INTENTION

In order to fully extend ourselves to others, we must first focus on our own selves. **Ask yourself: How do I show myself compassion?**

MONDAY /

TUESDAY /

WEDNESDAY /

THURSDAY / _____

_____

_____

_____

_____

_____

FRIDAY / _____

_____

_____

_____

_____

_____

SATURDAY / _____

_____

_____

_____

_____

_____

SUNDAY / _____

_____

_____

_____

_____

_____

My Done List

- ○ _____
- ○ _____
- ○ _____
- ○ _____
- ○ _____
- ○ _____
- ○ _____
- ○ _____
- ○ _____
- ○ _____
- ○ _____
- ○ _____
- ○ _____
- ○ _____
- ○ _____
- ○ _____
- ○ _____
- ○ _____
- ○ _____

The simplest acts of kindness are by far more powerful than a thousand heads bowing in prayer.
—Mahatma Gandhi

WEEKLY REFLECTION

How did I show compassion this week?

_____
_____
_____
_____
_____
_____
_____
_____

I practiced empathy when...

_____
_____
_____
_____
_____
_____
_____
_____

How could I have been more compassionate?

_____
_____
_____
_____
_____
_____
_____
_____

want to do more of...

_____
_____
_____
_____
_____
_____
_____

otes

_____
_____
_____
_____
_____
_____
_____
_____
_____
_____
_____
_____
_____
_____

MY INTENTION

To extend yourself in kindness to anybody is an expansion of kindness in the world. **Ask yourself: What is one random act of kindness that I could perform this week?**

MONDAY /

TUESDAY /

WEDNESDAY /

THURSDAY / _____ _____

_____

_____

_____

_____

FRIDAY / _____ _____

_____

_____

_____

_____

_____

SATURDAY / _____ _____

_____

_____

_____

_____

SUNDAY / _____ _____

_____

_____

_____

_____

My Done List

○ _____

○ _____

○ _____

○ _____

○ _____

○ _____

○ _____

○ _____

○ _____

○ _____

○ _____

○ _____

○ _____

○ _____

○ _____

○ _____

○ _____

○ _____

○ _____

○ _____

○ _____

> If you want others to be happy,
> practice compassion. If you want to be happy,
> practice compassion.
>
> —Dalai Lama

WEEKLY REFLECTION

How did I show compassion this week?

_____
_____
_____
_____
_____
_____
_____

I practiced empathy when...

_____
_____
_____
_____
_____
_____
_____

How could I have been more compassionate?

_____
_____
_____
_____
_____
_____
_____

want to do more of...

_____

_____

_____

_____

_____

_____

_____

_____

Notes

_____

_____

_____

_____

_____

_____

_____

_____

_____

_____

_____

_____

_____

_____

_____

MY INTENTION

In times of crisis or hardship, letting someone know that you care can be what sustains them.
Ask yourself: Is there a person in my life who needs encouragement right now? What can I do to support them?

MONDAY / _____

_____

_____

_____

_____

TUESDAY / _____

_____

_____

_____

_____

WEDNESDAY / _____

_____

_____

_____

_____

THURSDAY / _____

_____

_____

_____

_____

_____

FRIDAY / _____

_____

_____

_____

_____

_____

SATURDAY / _____

_____

_____

_____

_____

_____

SUNDAY / _____

_____

_____

_____

_____

_____

My Done List

- ○ _____
- ○ _____
- ○ _____
- ○ _____
- ○ _____
- ○ _____
- ○ _____
- ○ _____
- ○ _____
- ○ _____
- ○ _____
- ○ _____
- ○ _____
- ○ _____
- ○ _____
- ○ _____
- ○ _____
- ○ _____
- ○ _____
- ○ _____
- ○ _____
- ○ _____

A stranger's compassion can make a world of difference.
—*Oprah*

WEEKLY REFLECTION *Check-in*

I'm feeling compassionate toward:

I'm observing:

I'm struggling with:

I'm staying grounded by:

I want to better understand:

I'm happy for:

Notes:

MY INTENTION

One of the best ways to deepen your empathy is to put yourself in someone else's shoes.
Ask yourself: How can I put myself in someone else's shoes more often?

MONDAY /

TUESDAY /

WEDNESDAY /

THURSDAY / _____ _____

_____

_____

_____

_____

_____

FRIDAY / _____ _____

_____

_____

_____

_____

_____

SATURDAY / _____ _____

_____

_____

_____

_____

_____

SUNDAY / _____ _____

_____

_____

_____

_____

_____

My Done List

○ _____
○ _____
○ _____
○ _____
○ _____
○ _____
○ _____
○ _____
○ _____
○ _____
○ _____
○ _____
○ _____
○ _____
○ _____
○ _____
○ _____
○ _____
○ _____
○ _____

I'd been searching for ways to heal myself. I found that kindness is the best way.

—Lady Gaga

WEEKLY REFLECTION

How did I show compassion this week?

_____
_____
_____
_____
_____
_____
_____
_____

I practiced empathy when...

_____
_____
_____
_____
_____
_____
_____
_____

How could I have been more compassionate?

_____
_____
_____
_____
_____
_____
_____
_____

want to do more of...

_____

_____

_____

_____

_____

_____

_____

Notes

_____

_____

_____

_____

_____

_____

_____

_____

_____

_____

_____

_____

_____

_____

_____

_____

_____

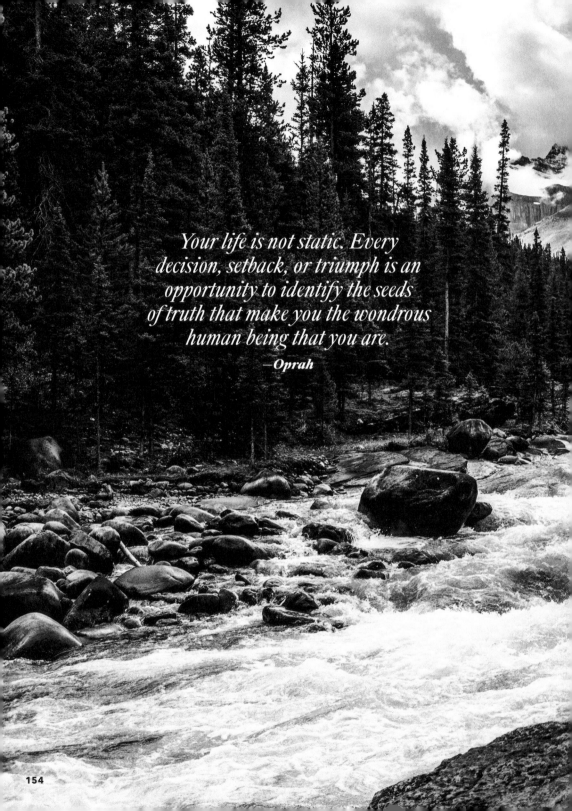

Your life is not static. Every decision, setback, or triumph is an opportunity to identify the seeds of truth that make you the wondrous human being that you are.

—*Oprah*

Forgiveness

For many people searching for peace and purpose, the greatest spiritual challenge they will ever face is the struggle to forgive. There was a time when I thought forgiveness was about the offender. I believed if I offered my forgiveness, I was accepting the person who harmed me, even condoning the act. But I've long since learned that releasing the pain, frustration, and anger you carry is a critical step toward freedom—for yourself. The truth is, if you're holding a grudge, that grudge is really holding you. Forgiveness doesn't mean that what happened to you is okay. It means letting go so that the past is no longer going to affect your present and your future.

—Oprah

What does forgiveness mean to me?

Who do I need to forgive?

How might my resentment and lack of forgiveness be holding me back?

How will forgiveness enhance my life?

MY INTENTION

When we are deeply hurt, offering forgiveness can seem easier said than done. **Ask yourself: What is my initial reaction to the concept of forgiveness?**

MONDAY /

TUESDAY /

WEDNESDAY /

THURSDAY / _____ _____

_____

_____

_____

_____

FRIDAY / _____ _____

_____

_____

_____

_____

SATURDAY / _____ _____

_____

_____

_____

_____

SUNDAY / _____ _____

_____

_____

_____

_____

My Done List

○ _____
○ _____
○ _____
○ _____
○ _____
○ _____
○ _____
○ _____
○ _____
○ _____
○ _____
○ _____
○ _____
○ _____
○ _____
○ _____
○ _____
○ _____
○ _____

Forgiveness is giving up the hope that the past could be any different.

—Dr. Gerald Jampolsky

WEEKLY REFLECTION

What steps have I taken this week to move toward forgiveness?

_____
_____
_____
_____
_____
_____
_____

What am I holding on to that I need to let go of?

_____
_____
_____
_____
_____
_____
_____

Is there anyone I need to ask for forgiveness? Why?

_____
_____
_____
_____
_____
_____
_____

want to forgive myself for...

_____

_____

_____

_____

_____

_____

_____

_____

Notes

_____

_____

_____

_____

_____

_____

_____

_____

_____

_____

_____

_____

_____

_____

_____

_____

MY INTENTION

_____

_____

Holding on to negative thoughts and emotions can negatively affect our well-being. **Ask yourself: How does holding a grudge impact my health?**

MONDAY / _____

_____

_____

_____

_____

TUESDAY / _____

_____

_____

_____

_____

WEDNESDAY / _____

_____

_____

_____

_____

THURSDAY / _____ _____

_____

_____

_____

_____

_____

_____

FRIDAY / _____ _____

_____

_____

_____

_____

_____

_____

SATURDAY / _____ _____

_____

_____

_____

_____

_____

_____

SUNDAY / _____ _____

_____

_____

_____

_____

_____

_____

My Done List

○ _____
○ _____
○ _____
○ _____
○ _____
○ _____
○ _____
○ _____
○ _____
○ _____
○ _____
○ _____
○ _____
○ _____
○ _____
○ _____
○ _____
○ _____
○ _____
○ _____
○ _____
○ _____

True forgiveness is when you can say,
"Thank you for the experience."
—*Oprah*

WEEKLY REFLECTION

What steps have I taken this week to move toward forgiveness?

_____
_____
_____
_____
_____
_____
_____
_____

Is it difficult for me to forgive someone who has hurt me? Why or why not?

_____
_____
_____
_____
_____
_____
_____
_____

Is it really possible to "forgive and forget"? Why or why not?

_____
_____
_____
_____
_____
_____
_____
_____

How do I know when I've truly forgiven someone? How do I feel?

_____

_____

_____

_____

_____

_____

_____

Notes

_____

_____

_____

_____

_____

_____

_____

_____

_____

_____

_____

_____

_____

_____

MY INTENTION

_____

_____

Forgiveness is essential for healing both ourselves and others. **Ask yourself: What is the relationship between love and forgiveness?**

MONDAY /

_____

_____

_____

_____

_____

TUESDAY /

_____

_____

_____

_____

_____

WEDNESDAY /

_____

_____

_____

_____

_____

THURSDAY /
_____
_____
_____
_____
_____

FRIDAY /
_____
_____
_____
_____
_____

SATURDAY /
_____
_____
_____
_____
_____

SUNDAY /
_____
_____
_____
_____

My Done List

○ _____
○ _____
○ _____
○ _____
○ _____
○ _____
○ _____
○ _____
○ _____
○ _____
○ _____
○ _____
○ _____
○ _____
○ _____
○ _____
○ _____
○ _____
○ _____
○ _____
○ _____
○ _____

Until you heal the wounds of your past, you will continue to bleed.

—Iyanla Vanzant

WEEKLY REFLECTION *Check-in*

I'm feeling:

I'm thinking about:

I find freedom when:

I want to accomplish:

I'm prioritizing:

I'm excited for:

Notes:

MY INTENTION

We all make mistakes, even when we have the best of intentions. **Ask yourself: Is there someone I need to apologize to?**

MONDAY /

TUESDAY /

WEDNESDAY /

THURSDAY / _____ _____

_____

_____

_____

_____

_____

FRIDAY / _____ _____

_____

_____

_____

_____

_____

SATURDAY / _____ _____

_____

_____

_____

_____

_____

SUNDAY / _____ _____

_____

_____

_____

_____

_____

My Done List

○ _____
○ _____
○ _____
○ _____
○ _____
○ _____
○ _____
○ _____
○ _____
○ _____
○ _____
○ _____
○ _____
○ _____
○ _____
○ _____
○ _____
○ _____
○ _____
○ _____

To err is human;
to forgive, divine.
—Alexander Pope

WEEKLY REFLECTION

What steps have I taken this week to move toward forgiveness?

_____

_____

_____

_____

_____

_____

_____

_____

When I ask someone to forgive me, what do I say?

_____

_____

_____

_____

_____

_____

_____

_____

What is one mistake I've made that allowed me to grow?

_____

_____

_____

_____

_____

_____

_____

_____

How do I practice self-forgiveness?

_____

_____

_____

_____

_____

_____

_____

Notes

_____

_____

_____

_____

_____

_____

_____

_____

_____

_____

_____

_____

_____

_____

_____

Renewal

One of the things that particularly excites me about springtime is when the first bright green shoots of baby grass start to emerge from the ground. The grays, browns, and whites of winter give way to vibrant bursts of color, bringing along new life and new beginnings. Spring is a time of renewal—from spring cleaning to spring break, we're encouraged to refresh both our surroundings and our spirit. None of us is built to run nonstop. That's why when you don't give yourself the time and care you need, your body rebels in the form of sickness and exhaustion. The idea of self-care may sound indulgent, but in order to fully give of ourselves to the people we love, we must create space to focus on our own restoration. Giving yourself time to just be is essential to fulfilling your mission as a human being. Whether it's a simple walk in nature or sitting out in the backyard, even five minutes of stillness can help re-center and refuel us for the week ahead.

—Oprah

What does it mean to me to relax?

What activities make me feel this way? How often do I do them?

What is one area of my health I'd like to improve?

Does putting my own needs first make me feel selfish or guilty? Why or why not?

MY INTENTION

Part of taking care of ourselves is engaging in activities we enjoy. **Ask yourself: What would make me happy right now?**

MONDAY /

TUESDAY /

WEDNESDAY /

THURSDAY / _____ _____

_____

_____

_____

_____

_____

FRIDAY / _____ _____

_____

_____

_____

_____

_____

SATURDAY / _____ _____

_____

_____

_____

_____

_____

SUNDAY / _____ _____

_____

_____

_____

_____

My Done List

○ _____

○ _____

○ _____

○ _____

○ _____

○ _____

○ _____

○ _____

○ _____

○ _____

○ _____

○ _____

○ _____

○ _____

○ _____

○ _____

○ _____

○ _____

○ _____

○ _____

You can't say "yes" to everything and not say "yes" to taking care of yourself.

—Shonda Rhimes

WEEKLY REFLECTION

How did I take care of my physical health this week?

_____
_____
_____
_____
_____
_____
_____
_____

I took care of my emotional health this week by...

_____
_____
_____
_____
_____
_____
_____
_____

I want to make more time to...

_____
_____
_____
_____
_____
_____
_____
_____

What brought me joy this week?

_____

_____

_____

_____

_____

_____

_____

Notes

_____

_____

_____

_____

_____

_____

_____

_____

_____

_____

_____

_____

_____

_____

_____

_____

MY INTENTION

When you nurture and support your mind and body, they reciprocate. **Ask yourself: What is one healthy habit I can start this week?**

MONDAY /

TUESDAY /

WEDNESDAY /

REMEMBER: Life is about finding balance, not perfection. Don't feel guilty for getting off track. Reset and start fresh tomorrow.

HURSDAY /
_____

My Done List

○ _____
○ _____
○ _____
○ _____

RIDAY /
_____

○ _____
○ _____
○ _____
○ _____
○ _____
○ _____

ATURDAY /
_____

○ _____
○ _____
○ _____
○ _____
○ _____

UNDAY /
_____

○ _____
○ _____
○ _____
○ _____

Nourish what makes you feel confident, connected, and contented.

—Oprah

WEEKLY REFLECTION

How did I take care of my physical health this week?

_____
_____
_____
_____
_____
_____
_____
_____

I took care of my emotional health this week by...

_____
_____
_____
_____
_____
_____
_____
_____

I want to make more time to...

_____
_____
_____
_____
_____
_____
_____
_____

What brought me joy this week?

_____

_____

_____

_____

_____

_____

_____

Notes

_____

_____

_____

_____

_____

_____

_____

_____

_____

_____

_____

_____

_____

_____

_____

MY INTENTION

This I know: More things don't make you feel more alive...in fact, they often clutter not only your space, but also your spirit and distract you from what really enhances your well-being. **Ask yourself: What can I donate, recycle, or throw away to de-clutter my life?**

MONDAY / _____

_____

_____

_____

_____

_____

TUESDAY / _____

_____

_____

_____

_____

_____

WEDNESDAY / _____

_____

_____

_____

_____

_____

THURSDAY / _____ _____

_____

_____

_____

_____

FRIDAY / _____ _____

_____

_____

_____

_____

SATURDAY / _____ _____

_____

_____

_____

_____

SUNDAY / _____ _____

_____

_____

_____

_____

My Done List

○ _____

○ _____

○ _____

○ _____

○ _____

○ _____

○ _____

○ _____

○ _____

○ _____

○ _____

○ _____

○ _____

○ _____

○ _____

○ _____

○ _____

○ _____

○ _____

Our physical, emotional, and spiritual health requires rest. We need to take a break.

—Dana Arcuri

WEEKLY REFLECTION *Check-in*

I'm currently feeling:

I'm reading/watching/listening to:

My favorite self-care activity is:

I'm motivated by:

To nourish my body, I'm eating/drinking:

Notes:

MY INTENTION

Making a change doesn't always mean starting something new—sometimes it's what we need to stop doing. **Ask yourself: What is one unhealthy habit I can let go of this week?**

MONDAY /

TUESDAY /

WEDNESDAY /

REMEMBER: Give yourself permission to rest when progress feels out of reach—you'll be better able to focus and achieve when you return.

THURSDAY / _____

_____

_____

_____

_____

_____

FRIDAY / _____

_____

_____

_____

_____

_____

SATURDAY / _____

_____

_____

_____

_____

SUNDAY / _____

_____

_____

_____

_____

My Done List

○ _____
○ _____
○ _____
○ _____
○ _____
○ _____
○ _____
○ _____
○ _____
○ _____
○ _____
○ _____
○ _____
○ _____
○ _____
○ _____
○ _____
○ _____
○ _____
○ _____
○ _____

To love oneself is the beginning of a lifelong romance.
—Oscar Wilde

WEEKLY REFLECTION

How did I take care of my physical health this week?

_____
_____
_____
_____
_____
_____
_____
_____

I took care of my emotional health this week by...

_____
_____
_____
_____
_____
_____
_____

I want to make more time to...

_____
_____
_____
_____
_____
_____
_____
_____

What brought me joy this week?

Notes

MY INTENTION

Creating the life you want means spending time doing the things that keep you fulfilled.
Ask yourself: What do I want to do more of this week?

MONDAY /

TUESDAY /

WEDNESDAY /

HURSDAY / _____ _____

_____

_____

_____

_____

RIDAY / _____ _____

_____

_____

_____

_____

ATURDAY / _____ _____

_____

_____

_____

_____

UNDAY / _____ _____

_____

_____

_____

_____

My Done List

○ _____

○ _____

○ _____

○ _____

○ _____

○ _____

○ _____

○ _____

○ _____

○ _____

○ _____

○ _____

○ _____

○ _____

○ _____

○ _____

○ _____

○ _____

If you don't love yourself, nobody will. Not only that, you won't be good at loving anyone else. Loving starts with the self.

—Wayne Dyer

WEEKLY REFLECTION

How did I take care of my physical health this week?

_____
_____
_____
_____
_____
_____
_____
_____

I took care of my emotional health this week by...

_____
_____
_____
_____
_____
_____
_____
_____

I want to make more time to...

_____
_____
_____
_____
_____
_____
_____
_____

What brought me joy this week?

_____

_____

_____

_____

_____

_____

_____

Notes

_____

_____

_____

_____

_____

_____

_____

_____

_____

_____

_____

_____

_____

_____

_____

_____

Service

As far back as I can recall, my prayer has
been the same: "Use me. Show me how to take who I am,
who I want to be, and what I can do, and use it
for a purpose greater than myself." I truly believe that
the reason for my success and everything I have
is because I let myself be fueled by what my contribution
to the world could be. When you shift your
focus from success to service, your work will instantly
have more meaning. A grand gesture is not the
only way to be of service. I'm talking about committing,
every day, to a heartfelt, compassionate
approach to life. Ask yourself: How will I use my gifts
and talents in service to myself, my family,
my community, and the world? And then start living
from that intention. Shift your whole life's
paradigm to service and you will reap success.

—Oprah

What is the energy I want to bring to the world?

What causes or organizations are important to me?

What personal strengths and qualities do I have that could be used to serve others?

What do I want my legacy to be?

MY INTENTION

A life of service begins right where you are. **Ask yourself: How do I use my gifts, my talents, and who I am to better serve my family, my community, my world?**

MONDAY /

TUESDAY /

WEDNESDAY /

THURSDAY / _____

_____

_____

_____

_____

FRIDAY / _____

_____

_____

_____

_____

SATURDAY / _____

_____

_____

_____

_____

SUNDAY / _____

_____

_____

_____

_____

My Done List

○ _____

○ _____

○ _____

○ _____

○ _____

○ _____

○ _____

○ _____

○ _____

○ _____

○ _____

○ _____

○ _____

○ _____

○ _____

○ _____

○ _____

○ _____

○ _____

○ _____

Life isn't about what you have;
it's about what you have to give.
—*Oprah*

WEEKLY REFLECTION

How did I offer myself in service this week?

_____
_____
_____
_____
_____
_____
_____
_____

How did I benefit from the service of others?

_____
_____
_____
_____
_____
_____
_____
_____

What qualities do I need to develop to better serve those around me?

_____
_____
_____
_____
_____
_____
_____
_____

How did my actions align with my values?

_____

_____

_____

_____

_____

_____

_____

Notes

_____

_____

_____

_____

_____

_____

_____

_____

_____

_____

_____

_____

_____

_____

MY INTENTION

The dedication and passion of others can help guide you as you seek to discover your own unique calling. **Ask yourself: Who do I admire for their service to others? Why?**

MONDAY /

TUESDAY /

WEDNESDAY /

REMEMBER: Your talents make you valuable and unique. The more you improve yourself, the more you can help the world around you.

THURSDAY /
_____
_____
_____
_____
_____

FRIDAY /
_____
_____
_____
_____
_____

SATURDAY /
_____
_____
_____
_____
_____

SUNDAY /
_____
_____
_____
_____
_____

My Done List
- ○ _____
- ○ _____
- ○ _____
- ○ _____
- ○ _____
- ○ _____
- ○ _____
- ○ _____
- ○ _____
- ○ _____
- ○ _____
- ○ _____
- ○ _____
- ○ _____
- ○ _____
- ○ _____
- ○ _____
- ○ _____
- ○ _____
- ○ _____

Everybody can be great... because anybody can serve.

—Martin Luther King Jr.

WEEKLY REFLECTION

How did I offer myself in service this week?

_____
_____
_____
_____
_____
_____
_____
_____

How did I benefit from the service of others?

_____
_____
_____
_____
_____
_____
_____
_____

What qualities do I need to develop to better serve those around me?

_____
_____
_____
_____
_____
_____
_____
_____

How did my actions align with my values?

_____
_____
_____
_____
_____
_____
_____

Notes

_____
_____
_____
_____
_____
_____
_____
_____
_____
_____
_____
_____
_____
_____
_____
_____
_____

MY INTENTION

Each of us has something we can do right now that can make a difference in someone's life.
Ask yourself: What can I do today to make someone else feel better?

MONDAY /

TUESDAY /

WEDNESDAY /

HURSDAY / _____

_____
_____
_____
_____
_____

RIDAY / _____

_____
_____
_____
_____
_____
_____

SATURDAY / _____

_____
_____
_____
_____
_____
_____

UNDAY / _____

_____
_____
_____
_____

My Done List

○ _____
○ _____
○ _____
○ _____
○ _____
○ _____
○ _____
○ _____
○ _____
○ _____
○ _____
○ _____
○ _____
○ _____
○ _____
○ _____
○ _____
○ _____
○ _____
○ _____

Give your hands to serve and your hearts to love.

—Mother Teresa

WEEKLY REFLECTION *Check-in*

I'm currently feeling:

I'm learning:

I'm proud of:

I'm finding joy in:

Notes:

MY INTENTION

Wherever there is darkness, we have the power to bring light. Even one small candle can make the difference. **Ask yourself: What gives me hope?**

MONDAY /

TUESDAY /

WEDNESDAY /

THURSDAY / _____ _____

_____

_____

_____

_____

_____

FRIDAY / _____ _____

_____

_____

_____

_____

_____

SATURDAY / _____ _____

_____

_____

_____

_____

_____

SUNDAY / _____ _____

_____

_____

_____

_____

_____

My Done List

○ _____
○ _____
○ _____
○ _____
○ _____
○ _____
○ _____
○ _____
○ _____
○ _____
○ _____
○ _____
○ _____
○ _____
○ _____
○ _____
○ _____
○ _____
○ _____
○ _____
○ _____
○ _____

The best way to not feel hopeless is to get up and do something. Don't wait for good things to happen to you. If you go out and make some good things happen, you will fill the world with hope, you will fill yourself with hope.

—Barack Obama

WEEKLY REFLECTION

How did I offer myself in service this week?

_____
_____
_____
_____
_____
_____
_____

How did I benefit from the service of others?

_____
_____
_____
_____
_____
_____
_____

What qualities do I need to develop to better serve those around me?

_____
_____
_____
_____
_____
_____
_____

How did my actions align with my values?

_____
_____
_____
_____
_____
_____
_____
_____

Notes

_____
_____
_____
_____
_____
_____
_____
_____
_____
_____
_____
_____
_____
_____
_____
_____
_____

MY INTENTION

When making big changes feels overwhelming, remember that it's okay to start small.
Ask yourself: What is one goal I want to achieve this week?

MONDAY /

TUESDAY /

WEDNESDAY /

THURSDAY /

_____

FRIDAY /

_____

SATURDAY /

_____

SUNDAY /

_____

My Done List

○ _____
○ _____
○ _____
○ _____
○ _____
○ _____
○ _____
○ _____
○ _____
○ _____
○ _____
○ _____
○ _____
○ _____
○ _____
○ _____
○ _____
○ _____
○ _____
○ _____
○ _____

Tell me, what is it you plan to do with your one wild and precious life?

—Mary Oliver

WEEKLY REFLECTION

How did I offer myself in service this week?

_____
_____
_____
_____
_____
_____
_____

How did I benefit from the service of others?

_____
_____
_____
_____
_____
_____
_____

What qualities do I need to develop to better serve those around me?

_____
_____
_____
_____
_____
_____
_____

How did my actions align with my values?

_____

_____

_____

_____

_____

_____

_____

Notes

_____

_____

_____

_____

_____

_____

_____

_____

_____

_____

_____

_____

_____

_____

_____

*Transformation doesn't
happen unless you're willing:
It's your choice.*

—Oprah

Gratitude

Practicing gratitude has, quite simply, transformed my life. Over the years, whenever anyone looking to make a change has asked me, "Where do I begin? What can I do?" my answer is always, "Start with gratitude." I know for sure that when you focus on goodness, you create more of it, and acknowledging what you have and what you are grateful for completely shifts the way you see the world. It isn't always easy, but it is often when you feel the least thankful that practicing gratitude can offer much-needed perspective. Try to live in the space of thankfulness every day—and whenever you can't think of what to be grateful for, just close your eyes and feel your breath. Follow it in and out. And be grateful that you're still here.

—*Oprah*

What are five things I'm grateful for right now?

What do I appreciate most about my current season in life?

What's a hard life lesson I felt grateful to learn?

Who are the people in my life I am the most grateful for? Why?

MY INTENTION

Your body is truly a miracle. Think of everything it does in a day—just to keep you alive!
Ask yourself: What aspect of my physical health am I most grateful for?

MONDAY /

TUESDAY /

WEDNESDAY /

THURSDAY /　_____

_____

_____

_____

_____

_____

_____

FRIDAY /　_____

_____

_____

_____

_____

_____

_____

_____

SATURDAY /　_____

_____

_____

_____

_____

_____

_____

SUNDAY /　_____

_____

_____

_____

_____

My Done List

○ _____
○ _____
○ _____
○ _____
○ _____
○ _____
○ _____
○ _____
○ _____
○ _____
○ _____
○ _____
○ _____
○ _____
○ _____
○ _____
○ _____
○ _____
○ _____
○ _____

If the only prayer you ever say in your life is thank you, that will be enough.

—Meister Eckhart

WEEKLY REFLECTION

What simple thing made this week better?

_____
_____
_____
_____
_____
_____
_____

What experience made me feel grateful?

_____
_____
_____
_____
_____
_____
_____

Who am I grateful for? How did I express this gratitude?

_____
_____
_____
_____
_____
_____
_____

What in nature did I enjoy the most this week?

_____

_____

_____

_____

_____

_____

_____

Notes

_____

_____

_____

_____

_____

_____

_____

_____

_____

_____

_____

_____

_____

_____

MY INTENTION

_____

_____

There's nothing like the gift of laughter to help melt away the stress of the day. **Ask yourself: What makes me laugh?**

MONDAY /

_____

_____

_____

_____

TUESDAY /

_____

_____

_____

_____

_____

WEDNESDAY /

_____

_____

_____

_____

_____

REMEMBER: The challenges and struggles we face in our lives help us to more fully embrace the joys of our successes.

THURSDAY / _____

_____

_____

_____

_____

_____

FRIDAY / _____

_____

_____

_____

_____

_____

SATURDAY / _____

_____

_____

_____

_____

_____

SUNDAY / _____

_____

_____

_____

_____

_____

My Done List

○ _____

○ _____

○ _____

○ _____

○ _____

○ _____

○ _____

○ _____

○ _____

○ _____

○ _____

○ _____

○ _____

○ _____

○ _____

○ _____

○ _____

○ _____

○ _____

I believe what we focus on expands:
The more we celebrate gratitude,
the more blessings come into our lives.
—Oprah

WEEKLY REFLECTION

What simple thing made this week better?

_____
_____
_____
_____
_____
_____
_____
_____

What experience made me feel grateful?

_____
_____
_____
_____
_____
_____
_____
_____

Who am I grateful for? How did I express this gratitude?

_____
_____
_____
_____
_____
_____
_____
_____

What in nature did I enjoy the most this week?

_____

_____

_____

_____

_____

_____

_____

Notes

_____

_____

_____

_____

_____

_____

_____

_____

_____

_____

_____

_____

_____

_____

_____

_____

MY INTENTION

Even though we might try to do it all on our own, sometimes we need a little help from our friends.
Ask yourself: Who in my life deserves a big "thank you" and why?

MONDAY / _____

_____

_____

_____

_____

TUESDAY / _____

_____

_____

_____

_____

WEDNESDAY / _____

_____

_____

_____

_____

THURSDAY / _____ _____

_____

_____

_____

_____

FRIDAY / _____ _____

_____

_____

_____

_____

SATURDAY / _____ _____

_____

_____

_____

_____

SUNDAY / _____ _____

_____

_____

_____

_____

My Done List

○ _____

○ _____

○ _____

○ _____

○ _____

○ _____

○ _____

○ _____

○ _____

○ _____

○ _____

○ _____

○ _____

○ _____

○ _____

○ _____

○ _____

○ _____

○ _____

○ _____

Wear gratitude like a cloak and it will feed every corner of your life.

—Rumi

WEEKLY REFLECTION *Check-in*

I'm currently feeling:

The teacher I'm most grateful for is:

My favorite things to eat/drink are:

I'm finding beauty in:

I'm excited for:

I'm embracing:

Notes:

MY INTENTION

I'm often inspired to give to others by the ways in which others have given to me. **Ask yourself: What makes me feel appreciated?**

MONDAY /

TUESDAY /

WEDNESDAY /

REMEMBER: Rituals are important for stabilizing change in your life. Make gratitude a daily habit and celebrate the abundance all around you.

THURSDAY / _____ _____

_____

_____

_____

_____

_____

FRIDAY / _____ _____

_____

_____

_____

_____

_____

SATURDAY / _____ _____

_____

_____

_____

_____

_____

SUNDAY / _____ _____

_____

_____

_____

_____

_____

My Done List

○ _____

○ _____

○ _____

○ _____

○ _____

○ _____

○ _____

○ _____

○ _____

○ _____

○ _____

○ _____

○ _____

○ _____

○ _____

○ _____

○ _____

○ _____

○ _____

Let gratitude be the pillow upon which you kneel to say your nightly prayer.
—Maya Angelou

WEEKLY REFLECTION

What simple thing made this week better?

_____
_____
_____
_____
_____
_____
_____

What experience made me feel grateful?

_____
_____
_____
_____
_____
_____
_____

Who am I grateful for? How did I express this gratitude?

_____
_____
_____
_____
_____
_____
_____

What in nature did I enjoy the most this week?

_____

_____

_____

_____

_____

_____

Notes

_____

_____

_____

_____

_____

_____

_____

_____

_____

_____

_____

_____

_____

MY INTENTION

Gratitude changes your consciousness, allowing your life to open and expand. **Ask yourself: What am I grateful for at this very moment?**

MONDAY /

TUESDAY /

WEDNESDAY /

HURSDAY / _____ _____

_____

_____

_____

_____

RIDAY / _____ _____

_____

_____

_____

_____

ATURDAY / _____ _____

_____

_____

_____

_____

UNDAY / _____ _____

_____

_____

_____

_____

My Done List

○ _____

○ _____

○ _____

○ _____

○ _____

○ _____

○ _____

○ _____

○ _____

○ _____

○ _____

○ _____

○ _____

○ _____

○ _____

○ _____

○ _____

○ _____

○ _____

Whatever we are waiting for—peace of mind, contentment,
grace, the inner awareness of simple abundance—
it will surely come to us, but only when we are ready to receive
it with an open and grateful heart.

—Sarah Ban Breathnach

WEEKLY REFLECTION

What simple thing made this week better?

_____
_____
_____
_____
_____
_____
_____

What experience made me feel grateful?

_____
_____
_____
_____
_____
_____
_____

Who am I grateful for? How did I express this gratitude?

_____
_____
_____
_____
_____
_____
_____

What in nature did I enjoy the most this week?

_____
_____
_____
_____
_____
_____
_____

Notes

_____
_____
_____
_____
_____
_____
_____
_____
_____
_____
_____
_____
_____
_____
_____
_____
_____
_____

Joy

When was the last time you felt real joy?
You know what I mean: those moments when every
fiber of your being feels alive, energized, and
excited—a feeling that you're doing exactly what you
were meant to do. Over the years, I've learned
how to find joy in the little things: the first sip of a
hot cup of tea, reading a great book, or sitting in
silence watching the sunset. It's easy to get caught up in
the nonessential aspects of our lives and forget to
enjoy ourselves. But the truth is, you have the option
to choose joy this very moment. Decide to start
each day with fresh eyes, to see the world with renewed
wonder, and experience jubilance on every level.

—Oprah

When was the last time I felt real joy?

What does joy feel like in my body? How would I describe it?

What activities or people bring me the most joy?

What changes can I make to my life to find more joy?

MY INTENTION

It's easy to feel so bogged down by the length of our to-do list that we forget to take in the joy that surrounds us. **Ask yourself: What stands between you and a more joyful life?**

MONDAY /

TUESDAY /

WEDNESDAY /

THURSDAY / _____ _____

_____

_____

_____

_____

_____

_____

FRIDAY / _____ _____

_____

_____

_____

_____

_____

_____

SATURDAY / _____ _____

_____

_____

_____

_____

_____

_____

SUNDAY / _____ _____

_____

_____

_____

_____

_____

My Done List

○ _____
○ _____
○ _____
○ _____
○ _____
○ _____
○ _____
○ _____
○ _____
○ _____
○ _____
○ _____
○ _____
○ _____
○ _____
○ _____
○ _____
○ _____
○ _____
○ _____

Know the joy of doing what you love, and never stop pursuing it.
—Oprah

WEEKLY REFLECTION

Where did I find joy this week?

_____
_____
_____
_____
_____
_____
_____
_____

What did I do to bring joy to others?

_____
_____
_____
_____
_____
_____
_____
_____

I wish I spent more time...

_____
_____
_____
_____
_____
_____
_____
_____

What am I most looking forward to? Why?

_____

_____

_____

_____

_____

_____

_____

Notes

_____

_____

_____

_____

_____

_____

_____

_____

_____

_____

_____

_____

_____

_____

_____

MY INTENTION

The happy memories of our past can inspire us to seek out those feelings again. **Ask yourself: Was there a time in my life when I felt the most joy? What happened?**

MONDAY /

TUESDAY /

WEDNESDAY /

THURSDAY / _____

_____

_____

_____

_____

_____

FRIDAY / _____

_____

_____

_____

_____

_____

SATURDAY / _____

_____

_____

_____

_____

_____

SUNDAY / _____

_____

_____

_____

_____

My Done List

○ _____

○ _____

○ _____

○ _____

○ _____

○ _____

○ _____

○ _____

○ _____

○ _____

○ _____

○ _____

○ _____

○ _____

○ _____

○ _____

○ _____

○ _____

○ _____

○ _____

We cannot cure the world of sorrows, but we can choose to live in joy.
—Joseph Campbell

WEEKLY REFLECTION

Where did I find joy this week?

_____
_____
_____
_____
_____
_____
_____
_____

What did I do to bring joy to others?

_____
_____
_____
_____
_____
_____
_____
_____

I wish I spent more time...

_____
_____
_____
_____
_____
_____
_____
_____

What am I most looking forward to? Why?

_____

_____

_____

_____

_____

_____

_____

Notes

_____

_____

_____

_____

_____

_____

_____

_____

_____

_____

_____

_____

_____

_____

MY INTENTION

_____

_____

Savoring the simple pleasures of life is a great way to discover more joy. **Ask yourself: What is my favorite part of every day?**

MONDAY / _____

_____

_____

_____

_____

TUESDAY / _____

_____

_____

_____

_____

WEDNESDAY / _____

_____

_____

_____

_____

THURSDAY / _____ _____

_____

_____

_____

_____

FRIDAY / _____ _____

_____

_____

_____

_____

SATURDAY / _____ _____

_____

_____

_____

_____

SUNDAY / _____ _____

_____

_____

_____

_____

My Done List

○ _____
○ _____
○ _____
○ _____
○ _____
○ _____
○ _____
○ _____
○ _____
○ _____
○ _____
○ _____
○ _____
○ _____
○ _____
○ _____
○ _____
○ _____
○ _____
○ _____

When we are centered in joy, we attain our wisdom.

—Marianne Williamson

WEEKLY REFLECTION *Check-in*

I'm currently feeling:

I'm trying to change:

I'm reading/watching/listening to:

I'm committed to:

I find the most pleasure in:

Notes:

MY INTENTION

If you want more joy, focus on what you love! **Ask yourself: What is something I'd do every day if I could?**

MONDAY /

TUESDAY /

WEDNESDAY /

THURSDAY / _____ _____

_____

_____

_____

_____

_____

FRIDAY / _____ _____

_____

_____

_____

_____

_____

SATURDAY / _____ _____

_____

_____

_____

_____

_____

SUNDAY / _____ _____

_____

_____

_____

_____

_____

My Done List

- ○ _____
- ○ _____
- ○ _____
- ○ _____
- ○ _____
- ○ _____
- ○ _____
- ○ _____
- ○ _____
- ○ _____
- ○ _____
- ○ _____
- ○ _____
- ○ _____
- ○ _____
- ○ _____
- ○ _____
- ○ _____
- ○ _____

Life is to be enjoyed, not simply endured. Pleasure and goodness and joy support the pursuit of survival.

—Willard Gaylin

WEEKLY REFLECTION

Where did I find joy this week?

_____
_____
_____
_____
_____
_____
_____

What did I do to bring joy to others?

_____
_____
_____
_____
_____
_____
_____

I wish I spent more time...

_____
_____
_____
_____
_____
_____
_____

What am I most looking forward to? Why?

_____

_____

_____

_____

_____

_____

_____

Notes

_____

_____

_____

_____

_____

_____

_____

_____

_____

_____

_____

_____

_____

_____

_____

_____

_____

Reflection

For me, one of the most delightful parts about keeping a
journal is looking back at its pages. Reflecting on the thoughts,
feelings, and ideas of the past allows me to see how
much I've grown and reminds me of everything I still want
to be. Life is about recalibrating, about continually
asking yourself: "What do I have to do to fulfill my purpose?"
"How do I create the life I want?" Learning to appreciate
your best lessons, mistakes, and setbacks as stepping stones to
the future is a clear sign you're moving in the right
direction and letting in the light. Since the day when the late
Gene Siskel asked me, "What do you know for sure?"
and I got all flustered and couldn't come up with an answer,
I've never stopped asking myself that question. Now,
I'm turning the tables. Look back at the pages of this planner
and answer for yourself: What do you know for sure?

—*Oprah*

What is the greatest lesson I learned since beginning this planner?

What have I done over the course of these last months that I am especially proud of?

How have my priorities changed in the past year?

What do I know now that I didn't when I began this journey?

MY INTENTION

Love is all around and exists in all forms. **Ask yourself: What do I know for sure about love?**

MONDAY /

TUESDAY /

WEDNESDAY /

THURSDAY / _____

_____

_____

_____

_____

FRIDAY / _____

_____

_____

_____

_____

_____

_____

SATURDAY / _____

_____

_____

_____

_____

_____

SUNDAY / _____

_____

_____

_____

_____

_____

My Done List

○ _____

○ _____

○ _____

○ _____

○ _____

○ _____

○ _____

○ _____

○ _____

○ _____

○ _____

○ _____

○ _____

○ _____

○ _____

○ _____

○ _____

○ _____

○ _____

○ _____

Life isn't about finding yourself.
Life is about creating yourself.

—George Bernard Shaw

WEEKLY REFLECTION

How is my life aligning with my vision?

_____
_____
_____
_____
_____
_____
_____
_____

When did I act with compassion, empathy, or integrity this week?

_____
_____
_____
_____
_____
_____
_____
_____

How did I show vulnerability or resilience this week?

_____
_____
_____
_____
_____
_____
_____

How am I practicing self-care and being fully present?

_____

_____

_____

_____

_____

_____

_____

_____

Notes

_____

_____

_____

_____

_____

_____

_____

_____

_____

_____

_____

_____

_____

_____

_____

_____

MY INTENTION

We all have a family we are born into...and a family we choose. **Ask yourself: What do I know for sure about family?**

MONDAY /

TUESDAY /

WEDNESDAY /

REMEMBER: You are worthy of praise from yourself and others. Acknowledge and celebrate the work you are doing to become the best version of yourself.

THURSDAY /

_____

_____

_____

_____

_____

FRIDAY /

_____

_____

_____

_____

_____

SATURDAY /

_____

_____

_____

_____

_____

SUNDAY /

_____

_____

_____

_____

_____

My Done List

○ _____

○ _____

○ _____

○ _____

○ _____

○ _____

○ _____

○ _____

○ _____

○ _____

○ _____

○ _____

○ _____

○ _____

○ _____

○ _____

○ _____

○ _____

○ _____

○ _____

○ _____

○ _____

Don't ask yourself what the world needs. Ask yourself what makes you come alive and then go do that, because what the world needs is people who have come alive.

—Howard Thurman

WEEKLY REFLECTION

How is my life aligning with my vision?

_____
_____
_____
_____
_____
_____
_____
_____

When did I act with compassion, empathy, or integrity this week?

_____
_____
_____
_____
_____
_____
_____
_____

How did I show vulnerability or resilience this week?

_____
_____
_____
_____
_____
_____
_____
_____

How am I practicing self-care and being fully present?

Notes

MY INTENTION

We're not meant to be stagnant; in order to become our best selves, we must continually move forward. **Ask yourself: What do I know for sure about growth?**

MONDAY /

TUESDAY /

WEDNESDAY /

THURSDAY / _____ _____

_____

_____

_____

_____

_____

_____

FRIDAY / _____ _____

_____

_____

_____

_____

_____

_____

SATURDAY / _____ _____

_____

_____

_____

_____

_____

_____

SUNDAY / _____ _____

_____

_____

_____

_____

My Done List

○ _____

○ _____

○ _____

○ _____

○ _____

○ _____

○ _____

○ _____

○ _____

○ _____

○ _____

○ _____

○ _____

○ _____

○ _____

○ _____

○ _____

○ _____

○ _____

○ _____

○ _____

Whatever you do in life...think higher, feel deeper. Life is not a fist. Life is an open hand waiting for some other hand to enter it in friendship.

—Elie Wiesel

WEEKLY REFLECTION *Check-in*

I'm currently feeling:

I can't imagine living without:

My favorite way to spend the day is:

I'm surprised by:

The words I'd like to live by are:

I want to celebrate:

Notes:

MY INTENTION

We are all responsible for our own life—it's ours to design. **Ask yourself: What do I know for sure about my future?**

MONDAY /

TUESDAY /

WEDNESDAY /

HURSDAY / _____ _____
_____
_____
_____
_____
_____
_____

RIDAY / _____ _____
_____
_____
_____
_____
_____
_____

ATURDAY / _____ _____
_____
_____
_____
_____
_____
_____

UNDAY / _____ _____
_____
_____
_____
_____
_____

My Done List

○ _____
○ _____
○ _____
○ _____
○ _____
○ _____
○ _____
○ _____
○ _____
○ _____
○ _____
○ _____
○ _____
○ _____
○ _____
○ _____
○ _____
○ _____
○ _____
○ _____

What I know for sure is that no matter how much wealth you
come to possess, everything passes and changes with time.
What is real, what is forever, is who you are and what you are
meant to share with the world. That is your true treasure.

—Oprah

WEEKLY REFLECTION

How is my life aligning with my vision?

_____
_____
_____
_____
_____
_____
_____
_____

When did I act with compassion, empathy, or integrity this week?

_____
_____
_____
_____
_____
_____
_____
_____

How did I show vulnerability or resilience this week?

_____
_____
_____
_____
_____
_____
_____
_____

How am I practicing self-care and being fully present?

_____
_____
_____
_____
_____
_____
_____
_____

Notes

_____
_____
_____
_____
_____
_____
_____
_____
_____
_____
_____
_____
_____
_____
_____
_____

*I've come to believe that each of us
has a personal calling that's as unique
as a fingerprint—and that the
best way to succeed is to discover what
you love and then find a way to
offer it to others in the form of service,
working hard, and also allowing
the energy of your life force to lead you.*

—Oprah

Fulfilling Your *Purpose*

I believe every one of us is born with a purpose. No matter who you are, what you do, or how far you think you have to go, you have been tapped by a force greater than yourself to step into a supreme moment of destiny, the reason you are here on earth. We are all worthy, and each of us has a contribution to make to the whole of humanity. The real work of our lives is to figure out what that purpose is and get about the business of fulfilling it in our own unique way. If you look back through the pages of this planner to your thoughtful responses, you will see a thread that connects and illuminates what is meaningful in your life. Therein lies your purpose. There is no greater gift you can give or receive than to honor your calling. It's why you were born. And how you become most truly alive.

After spending the past year cultivating a deeper, more meaningful connection to the world, think about how you can take what you've learned and use it to reinforce your own true calling.

—Oprah

What do I believe is possible in my life?

_____

_____

_____

_____

_____

_____

What am I passionate about? What makes me feel the most connected to myself and the world?

_____

_____

_____

_____

_____

_____

_____

What would I do if I knew I could not fail?

_____

_____

_____

_____

_____

_____

_____

Was there ever a time in my life when I felt like I was doing exactly what I was supposed to? What happened?

_____

_____

_____

_____

_____

_____

_____

PURPOSE BOARD

You're almost there! At the start of this planner, you created your ultimate "vision board" of your ideal life—declaring your dreams and goals to the universe. Now, after these past days, weeks, and months of thoughtful focus, think about where you want to go from here.

What do you know to be true about your life now? What do you still want to achieve? What is the lasting footprint you want to leave on the world? Use this page to write, draw, or paste what you believe you are meant to do while here on Earth. And remember—it's okay for your purpose to change as you evolve. Celebrate your growth and reflect on how far you've come.

CONGRATULATIONS!

Living your best life means showing up every day, embracing the present moment, and connecting with the deepest parts of yourself. Walking the path toward your highest self takes both courage and discipline, but I've come to know that as long as you are asking the right questions, the answers will always reveal themselves. As you look back at the pages of this planner, what do you see? Who do you want to be? How can you allow that person to emerge in all aspects of your life? These are the ultimate questions you get to answer with every action, thought, and feeling. I believe we are all here for a reason—but the only person who holds the key to unlocking that unique purpose is you. My hope is that the insights you've gained here have provided you with more clarity and direction as you discover all you're meant to be. I wish you love, peace, and freedom on your journey.

Oprah

For more inspiration and guidance on how to make living well a daily practice, visit **OprahDaily.com.**

Notes

Notes

Thank you

To re-order the planner and find more great products, visit
SHOP.OPRAHDAILY.COM

Unlock your Oprah Insider membership offer: OPRAHDAILY.COM

ENJOY ALL THE MEMBERS-ONLY BENEFITS OF OPRAH INSIDER, INCLUDING:

| Unrestricted access to digital content, including a 10-year archive of past issues of O, The Oprah Magazine | Exclusive newsletter including Oprah's "Weekly Intentions" videos, plus special deals and discounts | A year-long subscription to O Quarterly magazine | Members-only invitations to video livestream events with Oprah and Gayle |